Riches from Earth

BY JUDITH HODGE

Table of Contents

INTRODUCTION

What do you think makes life on Earth possible? Cars, computers, televisions, telephones? While these things are important, they are not the secret to our survival.

Earth's resources are what enable life to exist. Some of these resources can be easily seen. Others lie hidden deep beneath Earth's surface.

Earth's riches are found in many places. To learn about them, you are going to take an imaginary trip. Your guides on the trip will offer a new way of thinking about the riches of planet Earth.

Mini Ral

Digger Brown

Pete Roleur

Iggy Rock

Crystal Waters

SOIL

Are you prepared to get dirty? The first part of your trip takes you through the soil.

Pick up a handful of soil. The soil likely feels damp and loose. What do you see? You will probably find a few pieces of rock, some bits of clay and sand, and perhaps a few twigs or leaves. Soil also contains water and air.

Healthy soil is rich in **humus** (HYOO-mus), which is decayed plant and animal material. Humus releases **nutrients** into the soil. Plants use these nutrients to grow.

It might not look like it, but even the smallest handful of soil is teeming with life. In fact, more organisms live in soil than in any other habitat on Earth. Animals such as mice and snakes make their homes in soil. So do millions of ants, beetles, worms, and other bugs.

It's A Fact!

Without dirt, you would not exist! Plants get all the nutrients they need to grow from the soil. Soil also provides a place for plants to take root. Animals survive by eating plants or other animals that eat plants.

Soil is also home to forms of life too small to be seen with the unaided eye. If you look at a sample of soil through a microscope, you'll discover fungi and bacteria. They break down dead animals and plants into simpler substances that enrich the soil.

Earthworms act like small plows. They tunnel through the soil, helping to mix it. Worm tunnels act as passages for air and water.

One teaspoon of soil contains 10 billion bacteria. That's 10,000,000,000!

The soil is home to a huge variety of animals. Here are a few.

ant

centipede

In some places the soil is only a few inches deep. In other places it is a few feet deep. No matter how deep it is, soil eventually meets rock. More than 80 percent of soil comes from rock.

Chemicals in rock react with Earth's atmosphere. In time the rock surface wears away. Rain, wind, and ice play a part in breaking rock into smaller particles, too. When plants take root and grow, they help with the process. After many thousands of years, soil is created. Soil is a renewable resource; it is constantly, but ever so slowly, being formed.

Soil Profile

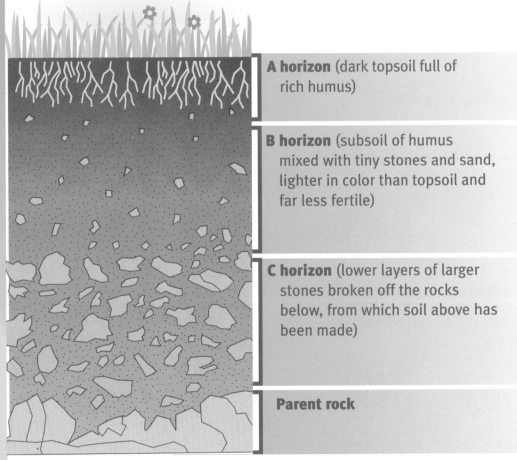

A horizon (dark topsoil full of rich humus)

B horizon (subsoil of humus mixed with tiny stones and sand, lighter in color than topsoil and far less fertile)

C horizon (lower layers of larger stones broken off the rocks below, from which soil above has been made)

Parent rock

Soil forms in layers known as horizons.

In the 1930s, more than 80 million acres of land on the Great Plains of the United States were damaged by careless farming and years of severe drought. The soil turned into dust and began to blow away.

Climate affects how quickly rock changes into soil. In regions where the ground is frozen for most of the year, soil builds up very slowly. In contrast, soil forms quickly in the warm, wet climate close to the equator.

It can take thousands of years for soil to form, but only a short time for soil to be destroyed by careless human use. Human activities such as logging and overgrazing speed up the natural process of **erosion**. Plant roots keep soil from being washed or blown away. When forests are cut down, there is nothing to hold the topsoil in place. Every year, millions of acres turn into desert when grasslands are overgrazed.

Even farming can harm the soil. Planting the same crop in a field year after year removes nutrients from the soil. This leaves the soil too poor in quality to grow plants.

Rocks

It's time to drill deeper into Earth and explore layers of rock. Rocks come in many colors, shapes, and sizes. Although there are many different rocks, they all fit into one of three main categories—sedimentary, igneous, or metamorphic. The category to which a rock belongs is determined by how it was formed.

The Grand Canyon was created by the weathering and erosion of red sandstone and limestone, primarily by the Colorado River. Can you see the different colored rock layers?

Sedimentary rocks are made from layers of sediment, or bits of sand, shell, rock, and other small pieces of matter. Sediments are carried by water, ice, and wind. When they are finally deposited, they form layers. The top layers press down on the layers below. In time, the layers become cemented together.

Rocks are not all the same. Rocks differ in size, age, and composition, to name just a few variations. Every rock—from a pebble on the beach to the rocks in the Grand Canyon—has a story to tell.

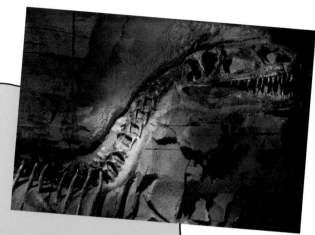

Rocks contain evidence that dinosaurs once existed. Dinosaurs lived on Earth for 145 million years before dying out about 65 million years ago. There are various theories about why they disappeared. Rocks hold important clues to the mystery!

Sedimentary rocks tell us much about Earth's past through the **fossils** they contain. When an organism dies, its remains are covered by layers of mud or sediment. The actual remains or a print of them may be captured in the sediment. When the sediment becomes rock, the remains or the print are preserved as a fossil.

By studying fossils, scientists can learn about living things, including those that are now extinct. Fossils also help scientists determine the age of the rocks.

activity

MAKE A "FOSSIL"
Fill a shallow box with sand. Make a hand- or footprint in the sand. Cover the sand with a layer of plaster of Paris. When the plaster dries, you will see a preserved print of your hand or foot. The plaster acts like a layer of sediment that hardens and forms a "fossil." Real fossils can be formed in a similar way.

Igneous rocks form the greatest part of Earth's hot interior. They are formed from melted rock, or **magma**, deep beneath Earth's surface.

Igneous rocks are formed in two ways. When magma cools and hardens deep inside Earth, igneous rocks are formed. Magma tends to cool slowly there, forming rocks that are "grainy" and textured.

Granite is an igneous rock that forms slowly beneath Earth's surface. It has a coarse texture.

It's good our clothes are fireproof. There's tremendous heat down here.

basalt

Obsidian and basalt form when lava from a volcano cools quickly. Obsidian cools so fast that it has a texture similar to that of glass. Obsidian is sometimes called volcanic glass.

obsidian

Magma reaches Earth's surface when a volcano erupts. This molten rock is called **lava**. When lava cools and hardens, it also forms igneous rocks. Lava tends to cool quickly at the surface, forming rocks that are smooth and fine-textured.

It's A Fact!

Pumice is formed when lava containing lots of gas bubbles cools on contact with air. The trapped air makes the rock very light— so light it floats in water.

11

Deep inside Earth, there is tremendous heat and pressure. When rocks are subjected to this heat and pressure, they can change into another type of rock called **metamorphic rock**. Metamorphic means "change of form."

Metamorphic rocks have properties unlike those of the rocks from which they were formed. For example, marble, a hard stone, forms from the sedimentary rock limestone. Marble is valued for its beautiful range of colors and textures, and for the ease with which it can be cut and polished.

Shale, a soft rock formed from mud and clay, changes into slate. Slate is used for roof and floor tiles. In the past, it was also used for blackboards.

The world's most famous marble comes from the Carrara mine in Tuscany, Italy. The Renaissance sculptor Michelangelo carved this and other statues from this marble. ▶

12

✔ P☺INT

Talk About It
Why is the study of rocks so important? Talk to a group member about this question.

These scientists are studying fossils at Dinosaur National Monument in Colorado to learn more about Earth's history.

The study of rocks has helped scientists learn about Earth's history. Scientists study rock layers to reconstruct the past. Fossils in different rock layers can tell us about land and climate changes.

Earth is about 4½ billion years old. We know little about the first 3 billion years because there are few fossils, and many of the rocks have changed more than once. This early period makes up 87 percent of Earth's life span. The last 590 million years are less of a mystery, thanks to the greater numbers of fossils that have been found in younger rocks.

MINERALS

You have just reached the center of a rock. Rocks are made of **minerals**. There are more than 2,000 minerals that naturally occur on Earth. However, most of Earth's rocks are made of only 30 of these!

Minerals are composed of **elements**, the basic building blocks of all objects on Earth. Some minerals, such as gold and platinum, contain only one element. Others, such as salt and quartz, contain two or more elements.

> ZAP!!!!!!!! Feel a little strange? Don't worry. You have just been zapped. You are now less than one billionth your normal size! You've gotten small enough to take a closer look at rocks. Follow me.

Granite, an igneous rock, consists mostly of two minerals, feldspar and quartz.

Most Common Elements Found In Minerals

oxygen
calcium
magnesium
silicon
sodium
aluminum
potassium
iron

Nearly 99 percent of minerals are made of a combination of just eight elements.

Minerals have many uses. They are used to manufacture computers, coins, jewelery, clothing, and glass. They are also vital to the proper functioning of the human body.

The minerals you eat when you have a bowl of your favorite breakfast cereal are the same minerals found in rocks! Your body needs as many as 80 minerals, but the main ones include iron (for blood), calcium (for bones), and fluorine (for teeth). Minerals enter the food chain through plants. In some cases, manufacturers add minerals to their products. This is true of cereals.

Important Minerals Your Body Needs

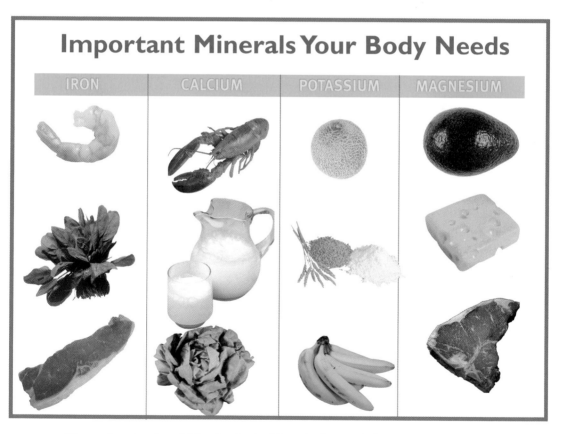

IRON	CALCIUM	POTASSIUM	MAGNESIUM

These foods should be included in a balanced diet because they are important to the proper functioning of the body.

All minerals are arranged in regular patterns called crystals. Crystals are solids that form when hot liquids deep inside Earth cool.

Crystals have definite shapes. Minerals can be identified by their crystal shape, as well as by their hardness, color, streak, luster, and the way they break.

Quartz is the most common mineral. Most grains of sand are quartz.

quartz

Minerals can be identified by their physical characteristics. These include color, luster, hardness, and crystal shape. Diamond, which is pure carbon, is the hardest mineral.

diamond   sulfur   mica

It's A Fact!

Hardness is a mineral's ability to resist being scratched. The German mineralogist Friedrich Mohs developed a scale of hardness in 1812 that is still used today. He chose 10 minerals as standards and graded them in order of hardness from 1 to 10, 1 being the softest and 10 being the hardest. A mineral can scratch those with lower numbers on the scale, but not those with higher numbers.

Sometimes the minerals from the Mohs scale are not available. In that case, a field hardness scale can be used. This scale is not as exact as the Mohs scale, but it can provide a general indication of the hardness of a mineral. Thus it can be used to identify the mineral.

MINERAL	MOHS HARDNESS	FIELD HARDNESS	
Talc	1	1	Easily scratched with a fingernail
Gypsum	2	2	Scratched by fingernail
Calcite	3	3	Very easily scratched by a knife; will not scratch a copper penny
Fluorite	4	4	Easily scratched by a knife
Apatite	5	5	Difficult to scratch with a knife; will not scratch glass
Feldspar	6	6	Scratched by a steel file;(6.5–7); may barely scratch glass
Quartz	7	7	May barely scratch a steel file; easily scratches glass
Topaz	8	8–10	Scratches a steel file
Corundum	9		
Diamond	10		

The different properties of a mineral determine its use. Graphite and diamond are both made of the element carbon. Graphite is soft and is used in pencils and lubricants. Diamond, which is the hardest substance on Earth, is used in industry and jewelry.

About 100 minerals are so rare and beautiful that they are given a special name—gemstones. Diamonds, rubies, and emeralds are gemstones. In their natural state, they are often rough and dull. Their rich colors and luster show when they are cut and polished. The hardness of most gems makes them good for jewelry.

Many gemstones form under specific conditions deep within Earth. It is only with the right temperature and pressure that these gems are created.

It's A Fact!

The world's largest diamond is part of the British crown jewels. It has a disappointing sparkle, however, because it was cut when tools and techniques were not very precise. How a diamond is cut affects its sparkle.

Gemstones include diamond, ruby, sapphire, opal, amethyst, topaz, jade, and citrine.

Many diamonds come from Kimberley in South Africa. They are found in a volcanic "pipe" that at its deepest reaches between 100 to 200 miles under Earth's crust. Of course, the diamond mines are not that deep.

Metals are important and useful minerals. Some, such as gold and copper, are found in their pure form in Earth's crust. Rocks that contain useful metals are called **ores**. They are collected from the surface of Earth or mined from deep underground.

Metals have many everyday uses. Copper is used for electrical wires because it is a good conductor of electricity. Iron is used in building materials because it is strong and durable. Metals can be melted and formed into many shapes. They can often be hammered or pressed without breaking.

Don't be fooled by this! It's pyrite, the main ore of iron. It looks like gold, but it's not. That's why it's often called "fool's gold."

FOSSIL FUELS

We need energy to provide heat and light, make machines work, run our cars, trucks, buses, trains, and planes, and generate electricity. In the United States, about 90 percent of the energy used comes from **fossil fuels**.

Fossil fuels are often found deep underground. When burned, they give off energy in the form of light and heat.

Fossil fuels formed hundreds of millions of years ago from the remains of dead plants and animals. The remains were buried under layers of sand and mud. Over millions of years, heat and pressure changed the layers into rocks and the plant remains into fossil fuels.

Fossil fuels provide most of our heat and light. We rely on them for about 90 percent of our energy needs.

Who would've thought that dead plants and animals could be so useful? If it weren't for fossil fuels, we would be without a major source of energy. You can see some of the fossil fuels here, thousands of feet underground as we continue our journey. They formed over millions of years. Be careful...it can be quite sticky here deep underground!

The three main fossil fuels are coal, oil, and natural gas. Fossil fuels are a nonrenewable resource. They cannot be replaced once they have been used up. Coal has been used as an energy source for thousands of years. It is a solid fossil fuel that develops in four stages. A different type of coal is produced at each stage. Each type can be used as a fuel.

Peat forms during the first stage. It is soft and brown and gives off lots of smoke but little heat when burned.

Lignite, or brown coal, is formed in the second stage. Like peat, it gives off small amounts of heat.

With added pressure, lignite becomes bituminous coal, the third type. This hard, shiny black coal, often called soft coal, is the most abundant type. The fourth type of coal is formed under enormous pressure. It is called anthracite, or hard coal. When burned, it gives off more heat than the other three types.

peat   lignite   bituminous   anthracite

Petroleum, or oil, and natural gas are often found together under layers of limestone and sandstone in areas that were once covered by oceans. Petroleum is a liquid fossil fuel. Natural gas, which is lighter than petroleum, is usually found floating above it. Oil and natural gas are obtained by drilling wells deep underground.

Oil that is removed from underground deposits is called crude oil. Crude oil is a mixture of many substances. It must be refined before being used. During refining, substances that are useful are separated and their impurities are removed.

Oil is used in industry to make many of the products you rely on every day. Oil is also used to heat homes, generate electricity, and power cars, trucks, trains, and planes.

For many years, natural gas was burned off as a waste product instead of being used. When its value as a heating and cooking fuel was recognized, it became popular as a clean source of energy. In the future, however, its limited deposits may cut down its use.

In only one day, humans use an amount of oil that took about 1,000 years to form! If we keep using fossil fuels at this rate, we may run out of them by 2080.

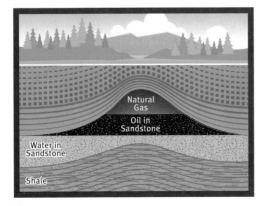

Natural gas and oil are often found in the same deposit. Natural gas is less dense than oil so it is usually found above the oil.

No one knows how long our nonrenewable resources will last. However, we do know that we will run out of them in time. Therefore, the conservation of energy is very important. Insulating buildings, driving fuel-efficient cars, using public transportation, and recycling materials are some of the ways people can reduce their energy use.

Many people are now looking into other forms of energy. Research is focusing on developing better ways of collecting, storing, and using the energy from renewable resources, such as the Sun, wind, tides, and the energy found within Earth itself.

It's A Fact!

The United States, with only 6 percent of the world's population, uses 25 percent of the oil produced in the world. An active conservation program could reduce consumption by half.

One alternative to fossil fuels is wind energy. Vast arrays of wind generators are used to produce electricity.

WATER

E arth is a watery planet. Water covers three-quarters of its surface. There is so much water on Earth that from space the planet looks blue!

Most of Earth's water, about 97 percent, is contained in oceans. Oceans are large bodies of salt water. The rest is found in lakes, rivers, ponds, underground springs, polar ice, and **water vapor** in the air.

It's now time to return to Earth's surface. The petroleum deposit you just visited is in the Gulf of Mexico. So you'll have to make your way up through the floor of the Gulf and into the water. Doesn't it feel refreshing? Water is Earth's most abundant resource, and one you couldn't live without!

DISTRIBUTION OF WATER

Atmosphere
0.0001%

Rivers, lakes
and streams
0.01%

Surface or
underground
0.6%

Fresh water
2.8%

Icecaps
and glaciers
2.2%

Salt water
97.2%

Water is one of the most abundant substances on Earth's surface. These graphs show the distribution of Earth's water.

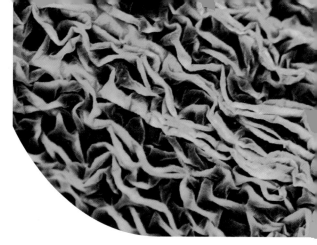

Water is home to microscopic algae, which produce most of the oxygen on Earth.

Not only does water make up most of the planet, it is also the main substance in all living things. The human body is about 65 percent water. An elephant's body is about 70 percent water. A tomato is almost 95 percent water!

Living things, including humans, need water because it is involved in all life processes. The human body needs to take in 2 ½ quarts (2.4 liters) of water a day in order to remain healthy. The water can be taken in directly from drinking or indirectly from foods we eat.

Water has many properties that make it essential for life. Water is known as a universal solvent. That means that many substances can be dissolved in it. You probably use this property of water every day. Beverages such as coffee, tea, lemonade, orange juice, milk, and soda contain substances dissolved in water.

This property makes it possible for nutrients to be carried throughout the body. The nutrients dissolve in water and are transported to cells, where they are used for growth and repair.

Water also dissolves and carries away the wastes produced by the body. Sweat and urine are made up mostly of water.

 POINT

Talk About It
People can live for two months without food, but only a week without water! How much water do you think you drink in a week? Talk about your answer with a group member.

Another important property of water is its **density**. Density is a measure of how much matter there is in a given amount of space. Density determines whether a substance floats or sinks in other substances.

Icebergs are large chunks of ice that break off glaciers. Only a small part of an iceberg is seen above the water. The larger part is hidden underwater. It's an unseen danger to ships. This fact is the derivation of the phrase "the tip of the iceberg."

Substances tend to be more dense in their solid state than in their liquid state. The exception to this rule is water. Ice is less dense than water.

Why is this important? Because ice is less dense than water, it floats in water. When bodies of fresh water begin to freeze, the ice that forms floats and creates a protective, insulating layer over the water. Plants and animals are able to survive through the winter in the water below. If ice was more dense than water, it would sink, not float. Bodies of fresh water would freeze from the bottom to the top, killing plant and animal life.

One of the most amazing things about water is that it can be found in nature in three different states. Water exists as a solid (ice), a liquid, and a gas (water vapor).

Water moderates temperatures on Earth. It takes a lot of energy to raise the temperature of water even one degree. For this reason, water can absorb and store a great deal of energy.

During warm seasons, water absorbs energy from the air, thereby lowering the air temperature. On cold days, water can release energy into the air, thereby raising the air temperature. In this way, water can influence temperatures.

Areas located on or near large bodies of water generally have more moderate temperatures than inland areas.

The Great Lakes formed 14,000 to 18,000 years ago when a huge sheet of glacial ice pushed down the land beneath it. As the ice melted, it filled the area with fresh water.

Glaciers tear out portions of land as they move.

Water is constantly shaping the landscape both above and below ground. Rainwater dissolves carbon dioxide from the air, forming a weak acid called carbonic acid. This reacts with minerals in some rocks. Over a long time, the acid can wear away a rock as hard as limestone. Water can carve out tunnels, caves, and underground rivers in some rocks.

Moving water shapes the land, too. As it flows downhill, it erodes the land in its path. At the end of its journey, it deposits huge amounts of sand and mud.

The powerful force of waves constantly wears away rocks.

The total amount of water on Earth never changes. It just keeps circulating in the endless water cycle. That's why water is a renewable resource.

People can harm the water supply by dumping sewage and chemicals into lakes, rivers, and streams. Fortunately, there is a growing awareness of the need to stop polluting Earth's water and to use it carefully.

Every glass of water you drink contains particles that have been used countless times before and will be used countless times again!

Clouds form when water vapor in the atmosphere condenses and collects.

The Sun's heat evaporates water from the oceans.

Water falls back to Earth as rain, snow, sleet, and hail.

CONCLUSION

The world is rich in resources. We have water and soil all around us and minerals and fossil fuels underground. Although some resources are plentiful and others are renewable, it is essential that we conserve all Earth's riches and use them wisely.

Can you think of ways you can conserve resources? Are you doing your share to protect the riches of Earth?

Many schools, supermarkets, and street corners have recycling bins where you can deposit glass, paper and cardboard, aluminum cans, and plastics.

GLOSSARY

density	(DEN-si-tee) the mass of a material divided by its volume (page 26)
element	(EL-e-ment) a substance that cannot be broken down into simpler chemicals (page 14)
erosion	(ee-ROW-zhun) the process by which sediments are moved from one place to another (page 7)
fossil	(FOS-il) the remains of a plant or animal, its shape, or a track preserved in rocks (page 9)
fossil fuel	(FOS-il fyool) a fuel, such as oil, coal, or natural gas, formed over millions of years from the remains of dead plants and animals (page 20)
humus	(HYOO-mus) a material in the soil that is rich in nutrients, produced by the breakdown of dead plant and animal tissues (page 4)
igneous rock	(IG-nee-us rok) a rock formed from liquid magma (page 10)
lava	(LAH-vah) magma that reaches Earth's surface (page 11)
magma	(MAG-ma) hot molten rock (page 10)
metamorphic rock	(met-a-MOR-fik rok) a rock formed from another rock that was changed by pressure or high temperature (page 12)
mineral	(MIN-er-ul) a substance found in the ground that has a particular chemical composition (page 14)
nutrient	(NU-tree-ent) a substance that provides energy and materials for growth and repair in an organism (page 4)
ore	(OR) a rock that contains a metal (page 19)
sedimentary rock	(sed-i-MEN-tu-ree rok) a rock formed from the settling of layers of sediments (page 8)
water vapor	(WAW-ter VAY-per) the gas form of water (page 24)

INDEX